SWIM

Dr. Peter R. Chambers
Illustrated by Gal Weizman

ISBN: 978-1-957723-34-1

Warren
publishing

Published by Warren Publishing
Charlotte, NC
www.warrenpublishing.net
Printed in the United States

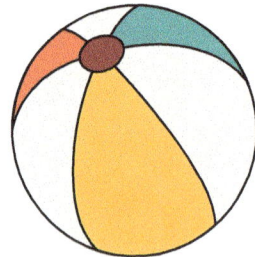

To the next generation of Watermen:
my great-nephews Bradley and Corin.
Already in the waves.

Everybody should learn how to swim.
But why?

First, and most importantly, swimming helps to keep you safe, both in and near the water.

And once you know how to swim, there are
a whole lot of fun sports and activities you can do,
some of which you may have never heard of nor seen.

- ✓ WATER POLO
- ✓ DIVING
- ✓ WATERSKIING
- ✓ SCUBA DIVING
- ✓ BOATING
- ✓ RECREATIONAL SWIMMING
- ✓ SYNCHRONIZED SWIMMING

GUARD

People of every shape, size, age,
and physical ability can participate in water activities.

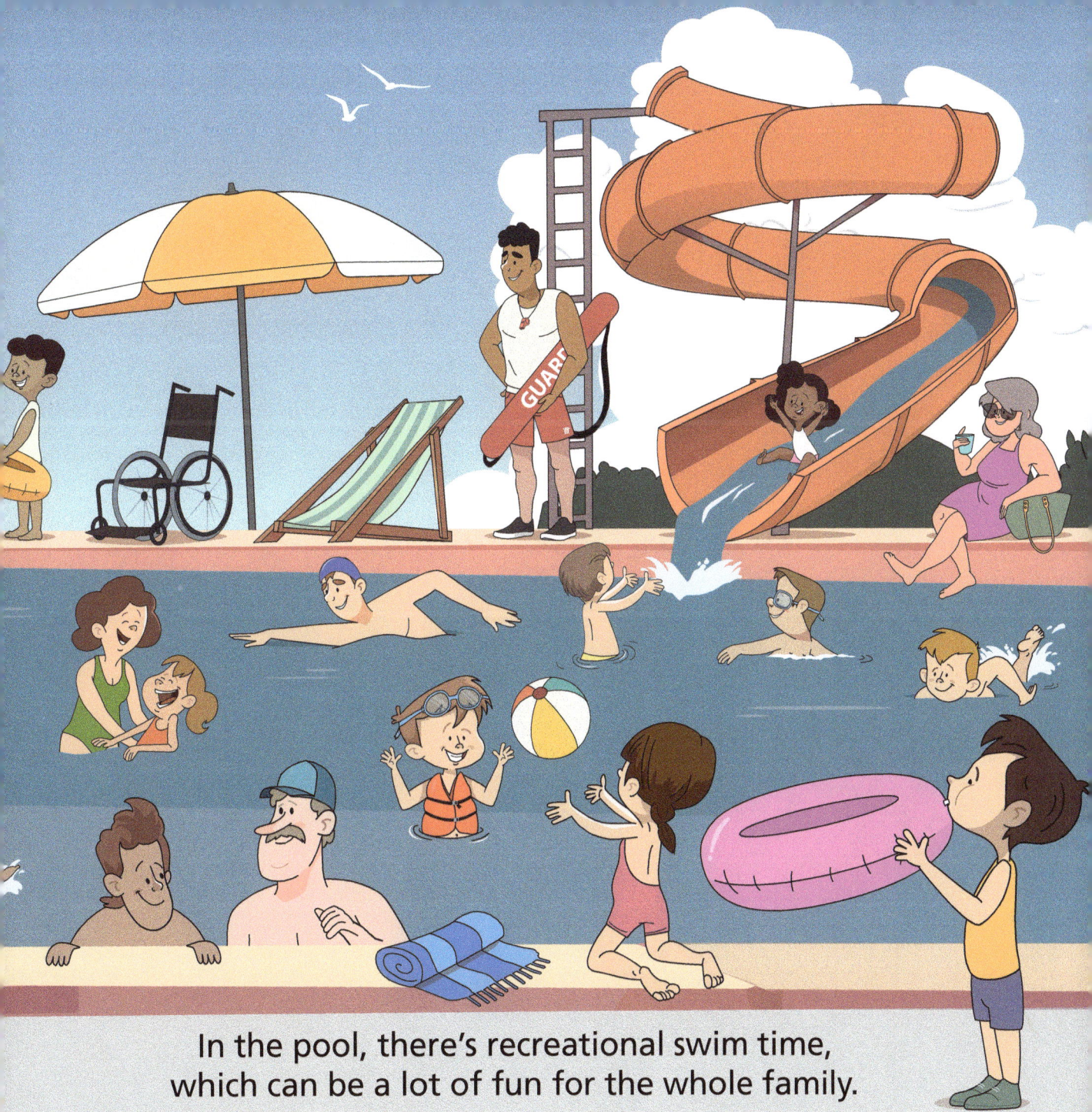

In the pool, there's recreational swim time, which can be a lot of fun for the whole family.

There are also organized sports like
competitive swimming where athletes race to the finish,

or water polo—a team sport that's action-packed!

Synchronized swimming is like
ballet in the water,

and diving is thrilling with its jumps, flips, and twirls.

The lake and ocean can be a lot of fun too.

There's open water swimming, like in a triathlon
where athletes swim, bike, and run!

Boating is a blast and provides so many options:
from the smallest sailboats to the largest ships.

Surfing can be exciting as you glide over the waves,

and body boarding is a cool hobby that's quick to learn.

You could try kayaking or canoeing, waterskiing, or kneeboarding.

Under the water, you can scuba and skin dive
as you explore the ocean's floor.

By the ocean, you can explore tide pools
with their many rocks, crags, and creatures.

And don't forget fishing, a fun and relaxing
way to spend the day.

Ready to jump in, head out, or climb aboard?

First, make sure you know how to swim! To learn or improve your swimming skills, visit your local YMCA, Red Cross, parks and recreation center, or swim school. Family and friends can be a big help too.

Practice hard and learn to swim in pools and open water. Experts say everyone should be able to swim 200 yards. Remember: it could save your life!

It's also important to learn water survival skills like swimming in cold water, swimming with your clothes on, and what to do if you get caught in a rip current.

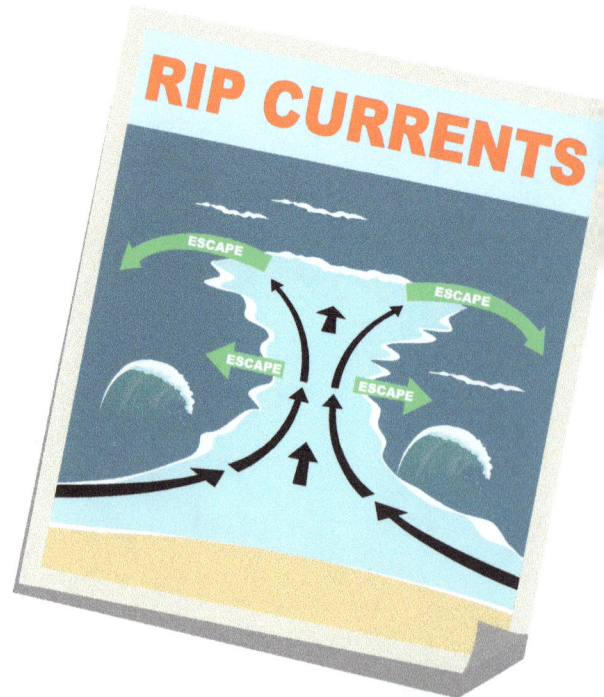

RIP CURRENTS

ESCAPE ESCAPE ESCAPE ESCAPE

Make sure you know your water lifesaving skills too.
Learn CPR and get familiar with using life jackets.
(And make sure to always wear your life jacket while
boating, jet skiing, or waterskiing!)

Be a Water Watcher: keep an eye on those around you.

And most of all …
always swim by a lifeguard!

So go out there, get in the swim of things, and have fun!

North Myrtle Beach Lifeguard Foundation logo

www.nmblf.org

All proceeds of this book will go to the
North Myrtle Beach Lifeguard Foundation,
a not-for-profit 501(c)(3) corporation
operating exclusively for charitable purposes,
specifically to promote water safety and ocean rescue.

ACKNOWLEDGMENTS

Thank you to the following for their commitment to water safety:
- The Department of Ocean Rescue North Myrtle Beach Public Safety
- The United States Lifesaving Association (USLA) leadership-past present, and future
- The American Red Cross
- YMCA
- Boy and Girl Scouts of America
- Swim schools
- USA Swimming
- ... And all swim instructors

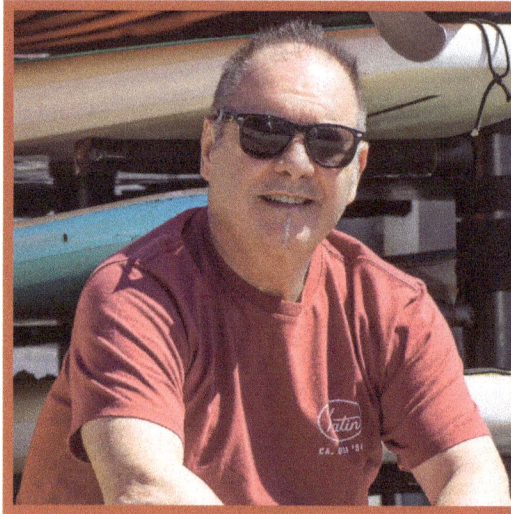

PETER R. CHAMBERS, PHD, DO
a.k.a. "Surf Doc"

When not in the water, Dr. Chambers is an emergency room physician. He is an open water lifeguard and serves as the medical director for the North Myrtle Beach Ocean Rescue in North Myrtle Beach, South Carolina. He is a true waterman, and a proud United States Air Force Veteran/Flight Surgeon.

Surf Doc's motto is to always
"SWIM NEAR A LIFEGUARD."

www.ingramcontent.com/pod-product-compliance
Lightning Source LLC
Chambersburg PA
CBHW051310020426
42331CB00018B/3494